ID0938595

MEDITATIONS FROM THE WILDERNESS

MEDITATIONS FROM THE WILDERNESS

Edited with an introduction by

CHARLES A.E. BRANDT

HarperCollins*Publishers*Ltd

*Photographs used on the section openers of this book were
taken by the author, Charles A.E. Brandt.*

The publishers acknowledge the invaluable research and expertise of Moira Dossetor.

Copyright acknowledgements begin on page 99.

http://www.harpercollins.com/canada

First edition

Canadian Cataloguing in Publication Data

Main entry under title:

Meditations from the wilderness

ISBN 0-00-255724-X

1. Nature - Prayer-books and devotions.   I. Brandt, Charles (Charles A. E.).

BV4810.M42 1997   242'.2   C96-931887-1

97 98 99 ❖ HC 10 9 8 7 6 5 4 3 2 1

Printed and bound in the United States

To my mother,
Anna Chester Bridges Brandt

CONTENTS

INTRODUCTION

The wilderness experience offers great riches. Those who write about the natural world often bring us a deep wisdom and, above all, a sense of hope. Their personal relationship with nature and their expression of it brings us all into deeper contact with the various dimensions of the universe, especially its spiritual dimension. This wilderness experience can be translated into one's lifestyle, into meditative prose and poetry, into song or dance.

Through communion with the natural world one comes to realize firsthand that the earth—its creatures, the galaxies, the universe itself—is a great celebratory event that, through a series of irreversible transformations, has brought us to our present moment, to the eve of a new millennium, to the threshold of the new age of the earth, an age Thomas Berry calls the Ecozoic Era. It is an age of great hope, unlike the terminal Cenozoic

Era which is drawing to its close. We name it terminal because of what we have done to the earth in our exploitation of it. But we can have hope that as we enter into this new age, we will see a transformation of human consciousness.

We will come to live fully in the present moment and embrace the spontaneities that the universe has poured—and is pouring—into us, that lead us into a loving relationship with the natural world and form a single, sacred community. Those who turn to the wilderness will enter into a deeper relationship with all beings as they learn to listen to the voices of these beings articulating themselves.

History indicates that such an earth–human relationship once existed. In the twelfth century, Francis of Assisi had such a relationship with the wilderness. He viewed the natural world as revelatory. There were two sources of revelation: the Holy Scriptures along with tradition, and the scriptures of the natural world. In the mid-fourteenth century when one-third of the population of Europe was decimated by the Black Death, mankind turned away from the earth, believing that it was being punished by God through the earth. Later, in the sixteenth and seventeenth centuries, when scientists such as Descartes, Sir Francis Bacon and Isaac Newton taught that—except for man's spirit—nature was purely a mechanism lacking any spiritual dimension, we lost what little relationship with the wilderness remained as we proceeded to control, utilize and exploit the natural world through the industrial revolution, the atomic and hydrogen bombs, and the development of nuclear energy. So today, we find ourselves working out of a human–divine, human–human set of relationships, to the almost total exclusion of a earth–human relationship. If we are to move into a meaningful sustainable future, it is necessary to bring the human community into a greater presence of the natural world in a mutually enhancing manner to form a single sacred community, as we once again establish a relationship of communion with the natural world.

Historically we have gone to the wilderness for different reasons. The early *rishis* went into the forest to offer sacrifice and to live in harmony with the universe. The early Christian hermits in the third and fourth centuries went into the desert of the Scete to practice perfect charity and constant prayer. Henry David Thoreau went to Walden Pond to find out what life was all about. Tom Merton went into the wilderness of Gethsemane to fulfill his need for solitude and to live a responsible "care-free" life. Aldo Leopold, the father of North American ecology, discovered in the Sand County of Wisconsin that he could no longer pose as one with control over nature, and that he was simply a member of the biotic community. As he underwent his conversion, he began to "think like a mountain."

In our own day, Thomas Berry and Brian Swimme are giving us guidance through their "Universe Story," the wilderness of the universe. They make it clear that if we wish to grasp this "New Story" we must first enter into communion with the natural world. We must come to realize that the natural world is a community of subjects to be communed with, not a collection of objects to be exploited. To do this, I believe, requires a transformation of consciousness. We must give birth to our deep, true self that lies waiting to be awakened. Indeed the greatest thing that we can do for the earth and for the universe is to become who we are.

Our ancestors, certainly as far back as 12,000 years ago and perhaps even earlier, gathered together to tell their sacred stories in caves, forests and in the longhouses of the northwest. They pondered the mysteries of the universe and the natural world: where did they come from and how should they relate to the universe? All cultures did this.

Today our North American culture does not, nor do most European cultures. We seem to have broken with the tradition that celebrates the universal mysteries. How are our children introduced into the universe today? The stories of the longhouse and the cave have been replaced by television. The action of the television show is driven by the advertisement. This new consumer society has debased our relationship with nature and therefore debased our culture. We no longer hear the voices of the natural world. We have become a society that is hard of hearing, an autistic generation. We hear what the consumer society wishes us to hear. It's not that we feel good about this. It has crept in unawares. We live with it. It has infiltrated our psyches, making us unhappy with our lives, our place in the universe, what we have. The natural world, through the media, has come to be seen more and more as a collection of objects without any spiritual dimension, a collection to be exploited and transformed into consumer items to fill up our emptiness and assuage our dissatisfaction.

How do we free ourselves from the tyranny of the consumer society? How do we discover our proper relationship with the earth? I suggest there are four ways to make this discovery: through a realized experience that we do live on the planet earth; through a deeper understanding of the "New Story" of the universe; through walking meditation; and through meditation that leads to a transformation of consciousness and the discovery and birthing of our deep, true self.

To deepen our relationship with the earth, we need to have some actual experience of living on a planet that turns on its axis every twenty-four hours and moves about the sun, which in turn is one of the millions of stars belonging to the Milky Way galaxy. We so often step out of our comfortable homes into our cars and travel to the shopping mall without any realization of all the wondrous activities our planet is involved in as it sails through space. A way to realize this activity is to go out just before sunset when the sun and perhaps the planet Venus are in the western sky. There will come a moment when you will feel, in a direct, experiential manner, the earth turning away from the sun. The experience will probably come suddenly, like a bolt of lightning. There will be a sense of awe and wonder as you realize that you are standing on the back of something like a giant mammal, turning ever so slowly and rolling through a vast ocean of time and space.

A deeper understanding of the universe story as narrated by Thomas Berry and Brian Swimme will enhance our relationship with the earth. Today, we find ourselves between stories. Not that we deny the old story. But we must be open to the "New Story," an empirical story from science that describes the irreversible transformations that have brought us to our present moment. As we begin to understand this story, we come to realize our own place and responsibility in the unfolding of the universe, and are filled with wonder and delight in the cosmogenesis that is ongoing and in which we are involved and contributing. It is a humbling thing to realize that the universe needs us.

Walking meditation is a practice and means of communing with the natural world. This practice is described by Thich Nhat Hanh in several writings. To practice walking meditation we simply place one foot before the other as we move through the wilderness. We have no destination. We allow our anger, frustrations and fears to fall away as we open ourselves to that which is. We discover a deep harmony and peace surrounding us.

Finally, we must learn to meditate, to become aware in an experiential way of our communion with ultimate reality. This is the relationship that we must develop with the natural world, a relationship of loving communion. As Ken Wilber puts it in *Up from Eden*,

And if we—you and I—are to further the evolution of mankind and not just reap the benefit of past humanity's struggles, if we are to contribute to evolution and not merely siphon it off, if we are to help the overcoming of our self-alienation from Spirit and not merely perpetuate it, then meditation—or a similar and truly contemplative practice—becomes an absolute ethical imperative, a new categorical imperative. If we do less than that, our life then becomes, not so much a wicked affair, but rather a case of merely enjoying the level of consciousness which past heroes achieved for us. We contribute nothing; we pass on our mediocrity.

Humanity is on the verge of a new and deeper level of consciousness, what we might call fourth-dimensional consciousness, which is simply living free from the pressures of time, or time freedom over clock time. It is living in the now. Indeed, this new consciousness seems already in orbit. It is only by embracing such a transformation of consciousness that we will begin to be freed from our small, exploiting, limited ego-consciousness so that we might realize our true communal relationship with all beings.

As a hermit monk living in a forested wilderness in British Columbia, on the banks of an as-yet-untamed river, not only do I open my eyes and ears and inner being to the sounds and sights of this Eden, but I open and expose my consciousness and human spirit to the resurrected, ascended, infinitely expanded human consciousness of Christ and, via a holy word, am carried by the loving action of the Spirit to the Father and thence to all beings in the universe, to discover a single loving community.

Charles Alfred Edwin Brandt

TANGLED ROOTS

The whole idea of compassion is based on a keen awareness of the interdependence of all these living beings, which are all part of one another and all involved in one another.

Thomas Merton

A thing is right when it tends to preserve the integrity, stability and beauty of the biotic community. It is wrong if it tends otherwise.

Aldo Leopold

I walked out alone in the evening and heard the birds singing in the full chorus of song, which can only be heard at that time of the year at dawn or at sunset . . . A lark rose suddenly from the ground beside the tree by which I was standing and poured out its song above my head and then sank still singing to rest. Everything then grew still as the sunset faded and the veil of dusk began to cover the earth. I remember now the feeling of awe which came over me. I felt inclined to kneel to the ground, as though I had been standing in the presence of an angel; and I hardly dared to look on the face of the sky, because it seemed as though it was but a veil before the face of God.

Bede Griffiths

With all beings and all things we shall be as relatives.

Black Elk

This earth which is spread out like a map around me is but the lining of my inmost soul exposed.

Henry David Thoreau

Every part of this soil is sacred in the estimation of my people. Every hillside, every valley, every plain and grove, have been made happy by some sad or happy event in days long vanished. Even the rocks, which seem to be voiceless and dead as they swelter in the sun along the silent shore, thrill with memories of stirring events connected with the lives of my people. And the very dust upon which you now stand responds more lovingly to their footsteps than to yours, because it is rich with the blood of our ancestors and our bare feet are conscious of the sympathetic touch.

Chief Seattle

The face of the land is our face, and that of all its creatures.

Linda Hogan

We are not the source of life, but are latecomers to the planet. Our minds didn't fall from the skies, but are the flowering of organic body and its capacities to know itself. We can touch our fellow beings and intuit the source of all life and thought that lies behind the whole.

Rosemary Radford Ruether

. . . a tree can tell us much in the language of its form, texture, age, and color and in the way it presents itself as an individual. But in this expression of itself, it is also showing us the secrets of our own souls, for there is no absolute separation between the world's soul and our own. We are truly the world, and the world is us.

Thomas Moore

We need the tonic of wildness—
to wade sometimes in marshes
where the bittern and the meadow-hen lurk,
and hear the booming of the snipe
to smell the whispering sedge where only some
     wilder and more solitary fowl builds her nest
and the mink crawls with its belly close to the ground
At the same time that we are earnest to explore
     and learn all things,
We require that all things be mysterious and
     unexplorable.

Henry David Thoreau

Let a man once begin to think about the mystery of his
life and the links which connect him with the life that
fills the world, and he cannot but bring to bear upon
his own life and all other life that comes within his
reach the principle of reverence for life . . .

Albert Schweitzer

The land bears witness to the way the elements trade places: it is limestone that floated up from the sea, containing within it the delicate, complex forms of small animals from earlier times, snails, plants, creatures that were alive beneath water are still visible beneath the feet. To walk on this earth is to walk on a living past, on the open pages of history and geology.

Linda Hogan

All over the earth, faces of all living things are alike. Mother Earth has turned these faces out of the earth with tenderness.

Luther Standing Bear

The indescribable innocence and beneficence of Nature—of sun and wind and rain, of summer and winter—such health, such cheer, they afford forever! . . . Shall I not have intelligence with the earth? Am I not partly leaves and vegetable moulds myself?

Henry David Thoreau

My eye catches the eye of a bird as it turns its head toward me on the side of the tree . . . My body, stretching in the sun, notices a tiny flower pushing up through the soil to greet the same sun. And we know our kinship as I and Thou, saluting one another as fellow persons.

Rosemary Radford Ruether

Many historical events, hitherto explained solely in terms of human enterprise, were actually biotic interactions between people and land. The characteristics of the land determined the facts quite as potently as the characteristics of the men who lived on it.

Aldo Leopold

Is not the sky a father and the earth a mother, and are not all living things with feet or wings or roots their children?

Black Elk

Humans discovered that the universe as a whole is not simply a background, not simply an existing place, the universe itself is a developing community of beings.

Thomas Berry and Brian Swimme

We come from the land, the sky, from love and the body. From matter and creation. We are, life is, an equation we cannot form or shape, a mystery we can't trace in spite of our attempts to follow it back to its origin, to find out when life began, even in all our stories of when the universe came into being, how the first people emerged.

Linda Hogan

Entire epochs are compressed in this solitary now. The past is here. Encoded in these rocks, in these trees, in the multitude of tiny lives that daily work this soil. Without the past there would be no soil, and without soil there would be no life.

Ken Carey

The material substances of our bodies live on in plants and animals, just as our own bodies are composed from minute to minute of substances that once were parts of other animals and plants, stretching back through time to prehistoric ferns and reptiles, to ancient biota that floated in the primal seas of earth. Our kinship with all earth creatures is global, linking us to the whole living Gaia today. It also spans the ages, linking our material substance with all the beings that have gone before us on earth even to the dust of exploding stars.

Rosemary Radford Ruether

This living flowing land
is all there is, forever

We are it
it sings through us —

We could live on this Earth
without clothes or tools!

Gary Snyder

My body is all sentient. As I go here or there, I am tickled by this or that I come in contact with, as if I touched the wires of a battery. I keep out of doors for the sake of the mineral, vegetable and animal in me.

Henry David Thoreau

Heaven is my father and earth is my mother and even such a small creature as I finds an intimate place in its midst. That which extends throughout the universe, I regard as my body and that which directs the universe, I regard as my nature. All people are my brothers and sisters and all things are my companions.

Chang Tsai

We are somehow failing in the fundamental role that we should be fulfilling—the role of enabling the Earth and the universe entire to reflect on and to celebrate themselves, and the deep mysteries they bear within them, in a special mode of conscious self-awareness.

Thomas Berry and Brian Swimme

. . . plants too are living organic beings that respond to heat, light, water, and sound as organisms, and even chemical aggregates are dancing centers of energy.
Human consciousness . . . should not be what utterly separates us from the rest of "nature." Rather, consciousness is where this dance of energy organizes itself in increasingly unified ways, until it reflects back on itself in self-awareness. Consciousness is and must be where we recognize our kinship with all other beings.

Rosemary Radford Ruether

EARTH LESSONS

Every part of nature teaches that the passing away of
one life is the making room for another.

Henry David Thoreau

Knowledge comes from, and is shaped by, observations
and knowledge of the natural world and natural cycles.

In fact, the word "god," itself, in the dictionary definition, means to call, to invoke. Like creation, it is an
act of language, as if the creator and the creation are
one, the primal pull of land is the summoning thing.

Linda Hogan

The spider's lesson is never to be greedy. It shows that objects of necessity can be objects of beauty and art as well. The spider also teaches that we can become too easily enraptured with ourselves.

Marlo Morgan

We all travel the milky way together, trees and men; but it never occurred to me until this stormday, while swinging in the wind, that trees are travelers in the ordinary sense. They make many journeys, not extensive ones, it is true; but our own little journeys, away and back again, are only little more than tree-wavings— many of them not so much.

John Muir

To go in the dark with a light is to know the light. To know the dark, go dark. Go without sight, and find that the dark, too, blooms and sings, and is travelled by dark feet and dark wings.

Wendell Berry

During the modern period and especially in the twentieth century, we have moved from that dominant spatial mode of consciousness, where time is experienced in ever-renewing seasonably cycles, to a dominant time-developmental mode of consciousness, where time is experienced as an evolutionary sequence of irreversible transformations.

Thomas Berry and Brian Swimme

Of all the interesting, strange and beautiful things I have seen and felt living here in the landscape, none have stirred and puzzled me more than my encounters with animals. I say "puzzled" for want of a better word: these encounters have struck a chord as deep as life itself, have opened up a darkness inside me resonant with knowledge that chooses to shape itself as questions rather than answers.

Sharon Butala

Animals and seeds do not honor the straight lines on human maps. They follow river beds, they migrate through mountain passes, they forage from mountain to plain, they pass from public forest to private, they blow where the wind blows.

David Bower

Beyond our genetic coding, we need to go to the earth, as the source whence we came, and ask for its guidance, for the earth carries the psychic structure as well as the physical form of every living being upon the planet. Our confusion is not only within ourselves; it concerns also our role in the planetary community. Even beyond the earth, we need to go to the universe and inquire concerning the basic issues of reality and value, for, even more than the earth, the universe carries the deep mysteries of our existence within itself.

Thomas Berry

As for mountains, there are mountains hidden in jewels; there are mountains hidden in marshes, mountains hidden in the sky; there are mountains hidden in mountains. There is a study of mountains hidden in hiddenness. An ancient Buddha said, "Mountains are mountains and rivers are rivers." The meaning of these words is not that mountains are mountains, but that mountains are mountains. Therefore, we should thoroughly study these mountains. When we thoroughly study the mountains, this is mountain training. Such mountains and rivers themselves spontaneously become wise men and sages.

Dogen

Unlike all the other flowers on land or in water, the lotus is the only flower that germinates and retains the seed until it becomes a plant. It is the only flower that does not die to start its own offspring. It completes the entire cycle of birth, life and death within itself. Humans, like the lotus, also reflect the continuity and cycle without ever totally being extinct.

Linda Gupta

The Native American peoples were especially distinguished for their sense of participating in a single community with the entire range of beings in the natural world about them. The drumbeat was experienced as striking out the rhythm of the Earth itself.

Thomas Berry and Brian Swimme

I went to the woods because I wished to live deliberately, to front only the essential facts of life, and see if I could not learn what it has to teach, and not, when I came to die, discover that I had not lived. I did not wish to live what was not life, since living is so dear, nor did I wish to practice resignation, unless it was quite necessary.

Henry David Thoreau

All birds, even those of the same species, are not alike, and it is the same with animals and with human beings. The reason Wakan tanka does not make two birds, or animals, or human beings exactly alike is because each is placed here by Wakan tanka to be an independent individuality and to rely on itself.

Okute (Teton Sioux)

The slithering snake is a learning tool when we observe its frequent removal of the outer skin . . . It is necessary to shed old ideas, habits, opinions, and even companions sometimes. Letting go is sometimes a very difficult human lesson. The snake is no lesser nor greater for shedding the old. It is just necessary. New things cannot come where there is no room.

Marlo Morgan

The present of our life looks different under trees. Trees have dominion . . . Trees do not accumulate life, but deadwood like a thickening coat of mail . . . We run around these obelisk-creatures, teetering on our soft, small feet. We are out on a jaunt, picnicking, fattening like puppies for our deaths. Shall I carve a name on this trunk? What if I fell in a forest: Would a tree hear?

Annie Dillard

Everything the Power of the World does is done in a circle. The Sky is round and I have heard that the earth is round like a ball and so are all the stars. The Wind, in its greatest power, whirls. Birds make their nests in circles, for theirs is the same religion as ours. The sun comes forth and goes down again in a circle. The moon does the same, and both are round.

Even the seasons form a great circle in their changing, and always come back again to where they were. The life of a man is a circle from childhood to childhood and so it is in everything where power moves.

Black Elk

My heart finds opening in these wetlands, particularly in winter. It is quiet and cold . . . Snowy egrets and avocets have followed their instincts south. The cattails and bulrushes are brittle and brown. Sheets of ice become windowpanes to another world below. And I find myself being mentored by the land once again, as two great blue herons fly over me. Their wingbeats are slow, so slow they remind me that, all around, energy is being conserved. I too can bring my breath down to dwell in a deeper place where my blood-soul restores to my body what society has drained and dredged away.

Terry Tempest Williams

If we had a keen vision and feeling of all ordinary human life, it would be like hearing the grass grow and the squirrel's heart beat, and we should die of that roar which lies on the other side of silence.

George Eliot

But ask now the beasts,
and they shall teach thee;
and the fowls of the air,
and they shall teach thee;
Or speak to the earth,
and it shall tell thee:
And the fishes of the sea
shall declare unto thee.

Job 12: 7–8

ONE BODY

It may be more appropriate to think of ourselves as a mode of being *of* the Earth, than a separate creature living *on* the Earth. Earth does not belong to us, it *is* us.

Elizabeth Roberts

The earth I tread on . . . is not a dead, inert mass; it is a body, has a spirit, is organic, and fluid to the influence of its spirit, and to whatever particle of that spirit is in me.

Henry David Thoreau

. . . your leg is part of our body. Well, so are the trees in the Amazon rain basin. They are our external lungs. And we are beginning to realize that the world is our body.

Joanna Macy

The whole universe is enhanced with the same breath, rocks, trees, grass, earth, all animals, and men.

Hopi Indian

The excitement of life is in the numinous experience wherein we are given to each other in that larger celebration of existence in which all things attain their highest expression, for the universe, by definition, is a single gorgeous celebratory event.

Thomas Berry

The world is your body.

Alan Watts

He who sees all beings in his self (*atman*), and his self in all beings, he loses all fear.

Upanishads

We know ourselves to be made from this earth. We know this earth is made from our bodies. For we see ourselves. And we are nature. We are nature seeing nature. We are nature with a concept of nature. Nature weeping. Nature speaking of nature to nature.

Susan Griffin

I am part of the rain forest protecting myself. I am that part of the rain forest recently emerged into thinking.

John Seed

It is the story of all life that is holy and is good to tell, and of us two-leggeds sharing in it with the four-leggeds and the wings of the air and all green things; for these are children of one mother and their father is one Spirit.

Black Elk

The human is less a being on the earth or in the universe than a dimension of the earth and indeed of the universe itself.

Thomas Berry

The rain forests of Brazil, and forests of the rest of the Earth, are the lungs of the planet, putting out oxygen and locking up carbon.

David Bower

You must ascend a mountain to learn your relation to matter, and so to your own body, for *it* is at home there, though *you* are not.

Henry David Thoreau

Modern man does not experience himself as a part of nature, but as an outside force destined to dominate and conquer. He even talks of a battle with nature, forgetting that, if he won the battle he would find himself on the losing side.

E.F. Schumacher

The entire earth community is infolded in this compassionate curve whereby the universe bends inwardly in a manner sufficiently closed to hold all things together and yet remains sufficiently open so that compassion does not confine, but fosters, the creative process.

Thomas Berry

CALM WILDNESS

. . . in God's wildness lies the hope of the world—the great fresh, unblighted, unredeemed wilderness.

John Muir

. . . in wildness is the preservation of the world . . . Life consists of wildness. The most alive is the wildest. Not yet subdued to man, its presence refreshes him . . . When I would re-create myself, I seek the darkest wood, the thickest and most interminable and to the citizen, most dismal, swamp. I enter as a sacred place, a *Sanctum sanctorum*. There is the strength, the marrow, of Nature. In short, all good things are wild and free.

Henry David Thoreau

How great are the advantages of solitude!—How sublime is the silence of nature's ever-active energies! There is something in the very name of wilderness, which charms the ear, and soothes the spirit of man. There is religion in it.

Estwick Evans

Each soul must meet the morning sun, the new sweet earth and the Great Silence alone!

Ohiyesa / Dr. Charles A. Eastman

We canonize old growth, but new wilderness is just as awesome—it testifies both to the beauty of Eden and the chance of redemption.

Bill McKibben

The pure land of Amitabha Buddha is said to have lotus ponds, seven-gem trees, roads paved with gold, and celestial birds. But to me, dirt paths with meadows and lemon trees are much more beautiful. As a novice monk, I told my master, "If the Pure Land does not have lemon trees, I don't want to go there." He may have thought I was stubborn. He didn't say anything.

Later I learned that this world and the Pure Land both come from the mind. That made me very happy. I knew that when you walk mindfully, you are already in the Pure Land.

Thich Nhat Hanh

I am in love with this world. I have nestled lovingly in it. I have climbed its mountains, roamed its forests, sailed its waters, crossed its deserts, felt the sting of its frosts, the oppression of its heats, the drench of its rains, the fury of its winds, and always have beauty and joy waited upon my goings and comings.

John Burroughs

Whenever the light of civilization falls upon you with a blighting power . . . go to the wilderness. Dull business routine, the fierce passions of the market place, the perils of envious cities become but a memory . . . The wilderness will take hold of you. It will give you good red blood . . . You will soon behold all with a peaceful soul.

George S. Evans

Climb the mountains and get their good tidings. Nature's peace will flow into you as the sunshine into the trees. The winds will blow their freshness into you, and the storms their energy, while cares will drop off like autumn leaves.

John Muir

From the forest and wilderness come the tonics and barks which brace mankind.

Henry David Thoreau

A certain Philosopher asked St. Anthony: "Father, how can you be so happy when you are deprived of the consolation of books?" Anthony replied: "My book, O philosopher, is the nature of created things, and any time I want to read the words of God, the book is before me."

Thomas Merton

This future will be worked out in the tensions between those committed to the Technozoic, a future of increased exploitation of Earth as resource, all for the benefit of humans, and those committed to the Ecozoic, a new mode of human–Earth relations, one where the well-being of the entire Earth community is the primary concern.

Thomas Berry and Brian Swimme

To the laborer in the sweat of his labor, the raw stuff of his anvil is an adversary to be conquered. So was wilderness an adversary to the pioneer.

But to the laborer in repose, able for the moment to cast a philosophical eye on his world, that same raw stuff is something to be loved and cherished, because it gives definition and meaning to his life.

Aldo Leopold

We need wilderness preserved . . . because it was the challenge against which our character as a people was formed.

Wallace Stegner

Only by going alone in silence, without baggage, can one truly get into the heart of the wilderness. All other travel is mere dust and hotels and baggage and chatter.

John Muir

To me, a wilderness is where the flow of wildness is essentially uninterrupted by technology; without wilderness, the world's a cage.

David Bower

Wilderness can be a means of reassuring ourselves of our sanity as creatures, a part of the geography of hope.

Wallace Stegner

. . . there is a love of wild Nature in everybody, an ancient mother-love showing itself whether recognized or no, and however covered by cares and duties.

John Muir

Now I hear the sea sounds about me; the night high tide is rising, swirling with a confused rush of waters against the rocks below . . .

Once this rocky coast beneath me was a plain of sand; then the sea rose and found a new shore line. And again in some shadowy future the surf will have ground these rocks to sand and will have returned the coast to its earlier state. And so in my mind's eye these coastal forms merge and blend in a shifting, kaleidoscopic pattern in which there is no finality, no ultimate and fixed reality—earth becoming fluid as the sea itself.

Rachel Carson

Man always kills the things he loves, and so we the pioneers have killed our wilderness. Some say we had to. Be that as it may, I am glad I shall never be young without wild country to be young in. Of what avail are forty freedoms without a blank spot on the map?

Aldo Leopold

When you lose contact with wildness, you've lost an important part of yourself . . .

David Bower

Now I see the secret of the making of the best persons. It is to grow in the open air, and to eat and sleep with the earth.

Walt Whitman

Indeed our individual being apart from the wider community of being is emptiness. Our individual self finds its most complete realization within our family self, our community self, our species self, our earthly self, and eventually our universe self.

Thomas Berry and Brian Swimme

Why should we be in such desperate haste to succeed and in such desperate enterprises? If a man does not keep pace with his companions, perhaps it is because he hears a different drummer. Let him step to the music which he hears, however measured or far away.

Henry David Thoreau

WONDERS
NEVER CEASE

What Nature is to the mind she is also to the body. As she feeds my imagination, she will feed my body; for what she says she means, and is ready to do.

Henry David Thoreau

The patches of bluets in the grass may not be long on brains, but it might be, at least in a very small way, awake. The trees especially seem to bespeak a generosity of spirit . . . We know nothing for certain, but we seem to see that the world turns upon growing, grows towards growing, and growing green and clean.

Annie Dillard

If we have a wonderful sense of the divine, it is because we live amid such awesome magnificence. If we have refinement of emotion and sensitivity, it is because of the delicacy, the fragrance, and indescribable beauty of song and music and rhythmic movement in the world around us . . .

If we have powers of imagination, these are activated by the magic display of color and sound, of form and movement, such as we observe in the clouds of the sky, the trees and bushes and flowers, the waters and the wind, the singing birds, and the movement of the great blue whale through the sea.

Thomas Berry

I was told, "Just as a musician seeks musical expression, so the music in the universe seeks to be expressed."

Marlo Morgan

At the moment, the governments of the world, certainly ours, value a tree only after it is cut down. But a tree has other responsibilities. Ask a bald eagle what the worth of a tree is. Ask a grizzly, who cannot prosper near roads cut into the forest. Ask the soil.

David Bower

In falltime you'll hear the lakes asking for snow to cover them up, to protect them from the cold. When my father told me this, he said everything has life in it. He always used to tell us that.

Richard K. Nelson

The water is one of earth's lanterns, the same blue of glacier light and of the earth from out in space.

Linda Hogan

This grand show is eternal. It is always sunrise somewhere; the dew is never all dried at once; a shower is forever falling; vapour is ever rising. Eternal sunrise, eternal sunset, eternal dawn and gloaming, on sea and continents and islands, each in its turn, as the round earth rolls.

John Muir

Extinction is a difficult concept to grasp. It is an eternal concept . . . A species once extinct is gone forever. The passenger pigeon is gone and will never return. So, too, the Carolina parakeet. However many generations succeed us in coming centuries, none of them will ever see a passenger pigeon in flight or any of the other living forms that we extinguish.

Thomas Berry

The creek is the mediator, benevolent, impartial, subsuming my shabbiest evils and dissolving them, transforming them into live moles, and shiners, and sycamore leaves. It is a place even my faithlessness hasn't offended; it still flashes for me, now and tomorrow, that intricate, innocent face. It waters an undeserving world, saturating cells with lodes of light. I stand by the creek over rock under trees.

Annie Dillard

Loneliness is an aspect of the land. All things in the plain are isolated; there is no confusion of objects in the eye, but one hill or one tree or one man. To look upon that landscape in the early morning, with the sun at your back, is to lose the sense of proportion. Your imagination comes to life, and this, you think, is where Creation was begun.

N. Scott Momaday

Consuming their own fallen leaves, they are nurturers in the ongoing formation of the world, makers of earth with a life-force strong enough to alter the visible face of their world . . .

Linda Hogan (on mangrove swamps)

Pollution, defilement, squalor are words that never would have been created had man lived conformably to Nature. Birds, insects, bears die as cleanly and are disposed of as beautifully . . . The woods are full of dead and dying trees, yet needed for their beauty to complete the beauty of the living . . . How beautiful is Death!

John Muir

Walking meditation is meditation while walking. We walk slowly, in a relaxed way, keeping a light smile on our lips. When we practice this way, we feel deeply at ease, and our steps are those of the most secure person on Earth. All our sorrows and anxieties drop away, and peace and joy fill our hearts. Anyone can do it. It takes only a little time, a little mindfulness, and the wish to be happy.

Thich Nhat Hanh

If I had influence with the good fairy who is supposed to preside over the christening of all children I should ask that her gift to each child in the world be a sense of wonder so indestructible that it would last throughout life, as an unfailing antidote against the boredom and disenchantments of later years, the sterile preoccupation with things that are artificial, the alienation from the sources of our strength.

Rachel Carson

Seldom am I without one or another of my dependents, even though they are not always visible. The crash of a new-fallen tree, or a shrill outcry of adolescent beaver voices from the lake, may disturb the sleeping echoes. The door is thrown open and a load of mud and sticks comes in, borne in furry arms and intended as materials for the earthen lodge that stands inside my cabin; then a light pitter-patter across the floor, as a muskrat calls in for his nightly apple; comes the rattle of antlers among the willows—these sounds, familiar to me as are street noises to a town-dweller, tell me that I am not, after all, alone.

Grey Owl

The forest and forest soil are the essential elements of the Earth's thin, dynamic, beautiful skin.

David Bower

How deep our sleep last night in the mountain's heart, beneath the trees and stars, hushed by solemn-sounding waterfalls and many small soothing voices in sweet accord whispering peace!

And our first pure mountain day, warm, calm, cloudless—how immeasurable it seems, how serenely wild! I can scarcely remember its beginning. Along the river, over the hills, in the ground, in the sky, spring work is going on with joyful enthusiasm, new life, new beauty, unfolding, unrolling in glorious exuberant extravagance—new birds in their nests, new winged creatures in the air, and new leaves, new flowers, spreading, shining, rejoicing everywhere.

John Muir

The universe we might consider as a single, multiform, sequential, celebratory event, as is implied in the designation of a flock of larks as an exaltation of larks, a title with implications of flight and song expressing delight in existence. For even the afflictions endured cannot diminish the songs that resonate throughout the natural world.

Thomas Berry and Brian Swimme

Living is moving, time is a live creek bearing changing lights.

Annie Dillard

I have seen the willets dancing in the springtime on the shore, dancing not only on the short salt grass that is covered monthly by the tide, but dancing in air, like butterflies, or salamanders wrapped in flame. This three-dimensional dance, a spiral reaching toward the sky, expands and replicates the helix that is at the core of life: the double spiral of the chromosome, the protean spirals of the albuminoids, the simplicity and perfection of the circle with the added dimensions of motion and time, the elements that make of all perfection a transience, a flowering and a becoming.

Harold Horwood

Winds are advertisements of all they touch, however much or little we may be able to read them, telling their wanderings even by their scents alone.

John Muir

Since water still flows, though we cut it with swords
And sorrow returns, though we drown it with wind,
Since the world can in no way answer to our craving,
I will loosen my hair tomorrow and take to a fishing boat.

Li Po

A lake is the landscape's most beautiful and expressive feature. It is earth's eye; looking into which the beholder measures the depth of his own nature. The fluviatile trees next the shore are the slender eyelashes which fringe it, and the wooded hills and cliffs around are its overhanging brows.

Henry David Thoreau

The mountain winds, like the dew and rain, sunshine and snow, are measured and bestowed with love on the forest to develop their strength and beauty.

John Muir

Beauty itself is the language to which we have no key; it is the mute cipher, the cryptogram, the uncracked, unbroken code.

Annie Dillard

I am particularly fond of the little groves of oak trees. I love to look at them, because they endure the wintry storm and the summer's heat, and—not unlike ourselves—seem to flourish by them.

Sitting Bull

. . . rapport with the marvelously purposeless world of nature gives us new eyes for ourselves—eyes in which our very self-importance is not condemned, but seen as something quite other than what it imagines itself to be. In this light all the weirdly abstract and pompous pursuits of men are suddenly transformed into natural marvels of the same order as the immense beaks of the toucans and hornbills, the fabulous tails of the birds of paradise, the towering necks of the giraffes, and the vividly polychromed posteriors of the baboons. Seen thus, neither as something to be condemned nor in its accustomed aspect of serious worth, the self-importance of man dissolves in laughter.

Alan Watts

There is a muscular energy in sunlight corresponding to the spiritual energy of wind.

Annie Dillard

Trees are alive and they have life like others because on cutting they feel sorrow. Similarly they have the feeling of happiness. After cutting a new branch comes out.

Mahabharata

The only true joy on earth is to escape from the prison of our own false self, and enter by love into union with the Life Who dwells and sings with the essence of every creature and in the core of our own souls.

Thomas Merton

LIVING
WITH RESPECT

Every step that we take upon you should be done in a sacred manner; each step should be as a prayer.

Black Elk (Prayer to Mother Earth)

If we can truly feel that we are part of, rather than apart from, our environment, then not killing is as natural as deliberately not stabbing ourselves with a knife; theft becomes as meaningless as stealing from oneself. Our relationship with our environment is a mutual caring. Morality then, is not a question of piously doing the right thing, but of being (and hence doing) what we truly are.

Buddhist writer

The naturalist must allow himself to be engulfed to his very ears in the odors and textures of sensible reality. He must become, like the muskrat, a limpid eyeball peering out of the sedges of a flooded meadow. By being fully immersed in his fluid environment as this sleek brown rodent, the naturalist could see his world with all his senses cleansed and alert.

Henry David Thoreau

We seek a renewed stirring of love for the earth
We plead that what we are capable of doing is
not always what we ought to do.
We urge that all people now determine
that a wide untrammeled freedom shall remain
to testify that this generation has love for the next.
If we want to succeed in that, we might show, meanwhile,
a little more love for this one, and for each other.

Nancy Newhall

"All men have the stars," he answered, "but they are not the same things for different people. For some, who are travelers, the stars are guides. For others they are no more than little lights in the sky. For others, who are scholars, they are problems. For my business-man they were wealth . . . you—alone—have the stars as no one else has them . . ."

"I wonder whether the stars are set alight in heaven so that one day each one of us may find his own again . . ."

". . . the stars, the desert—what gives them their beauty is something that is invisible!"

"And now here is my secret, a very simple secret: It is only with the heart that one can see rightly; what is essential is invisible to the eye."

Antoine de Saint-Exupery

Conservation is a state of harmony between men and land.

Aldo Leopold

Return to the land means recovering something of the biorhythms of the body, the day, and the seasons from the world of clocks, computers, and artificial lighting that have almost entirely alienated us from these biorhythms.

Rosemary Radford Ruether

I would insist that our love for our natural home has to go beyond finite, into the boundless—like the love of a mother for her children, whose devotion extends to both the gifted and the scarred among her brood.

Barbara Kingsolver

Man is but a part of the fabric of life—dependent on the whole fabric for his very existence. As the most highly developed tool-using animal, he must recognize that the unknown evolutionary destinies of other life forms are to be respected . . . There are now too many human beings, and the problem is growing rapidly worse. The goal would be half of the present world population, or less . . . Let reverence for life and reverence for the feminine mean also reverence for other species, and future human lives, most of which are threatened . . . I am a child of all life, and all living beings are my brothers and sisters.

Gary Snyder

Those who know do not talk.
Those who talk do not know.

Keep your mouth closed.
Guard your sense.
Temper your sharpness.
Simplify your problems.
Mask your brightness.
Be at one with the dust of the earth.
This is primal union.

He who has achieved this state
Is unconcerned with friends and enemies,
With good and harm, with honor and disgrace.
This therefore is the highest state of man.

Lao Tzu

For those persons who desire to follow the right course of conduct, there is no supreme dharma other than abstinence from violence to living beings caused by thought, word and deed.

Linda Gupta

Wisdom is intuitive knowledge of the mind of love and clarity that lies beneath one's ego-driven anxieties and aggressions. Meditation is going into the mind to see this for yourself—over and over again, until it becomes the mind you live in. Morality is bringing it back out in the way you live, through personal example and responsible action, ultimately toward the true community (*sangha*) of "all beings."

Gary Snyder

. . . time is the one thing we have been given, and we have been given to time. Time gives us a whirl. We keep waking from a dream we can't recall, looking around in surprise, and lapsing back, for years on end. All I want to do is stay awake, keep my head up, prop my eyes open, with toothpicks, with trees.

Annie Dillard

The changes we are dealing with are changes on a geological and biological order of magnitude. The four great components of the earth—the landsphere, the watersphere, the airsphere, and the lifesphere—are being decisively and permanently altered in their composition and their functioning by the most recent sphere, the mindsphere, altered, that is, in a deleterious, irreversible manner.

So long as we are under the illusion that we know best what is good for the earth and for ourselves, then we will continue our present course, with its devastating consequences on the entire earth community.

Our best procedure might be to consider that we need not a human answer to an earth problem, but an earth answer to an earth problem. The earth will solve its problems, and possibly our own, if we will let the earth function in its own ways. We need only listen to what the earth is telling us.

Thomas Berry

Our thoughts must be on how to restore to the Earth its dignity as a living being . . .

Beyond feeding and clothing and sheltering ourselves even abundantly, we should be allowed to destroy only what we ourselves can re-create. We cannot re-create this world. We cannot re-create "wilderness." We cannot even, truly, re-create ourselves. Only our behavior can we re-create, or create anew.

Alice Walker

When we see land as a community to which we belong, we may begin to use it with love and respect.

Aldo Leopold

We believe that the spirit pervades all creation and that every creature possesses a soul in some degree though not necessarily a soul conscious of itself. The tree, the waterfall, the grizzly bear, each is an embodied Force, and as such an object of reverence.

Ohiyesa / Dr. Charles A. Eastman

Someone in my childhood gave me the impression that fiddleheads and mourning cloaks were rare and precious. Now I realize they are fairly ordinary members of eastern woodland fauna and flora, but I still feel lucky and even virtuous—a gifted observer—when I see them.

For that matter, they probably *are* rare, in the scope of human experience. A great many people will live out their days without ever seeing such sights, or if they do, never *gasping*. My parents taught me this—to gasp, and feel lucky. They gave me the gift of making mountains out of nature's exquisite molehills.

Barbara Kingsolver

All ethics so far evolved rest upon a single premise: that the individual is a member of a community of interdependent parts . . . The land ethic simply enlarges the boundaries of the community to include soils, waters, plants and animals, or collectively, the land.

Aldo Leopold

The virtue of nonviolence is one of the greatest virtues as it is based on the deeper understanding of the kinship of nature. Developing one's humility toward all life forms is based on the oneness of all facets of nature.

Linda Gupta

We do not like to harm the trees. Whenever we can, we always make an offering of tobacco to the trees before we cut them down. We never waste the wood, but use all that we cut down. If we did not think of their feelings, and did not offer them tobacco before cutting them down, all the other trees in the forest would weep, and that would make our hearts sad, too.

Anonymous

We are capable of suffering with our world, and that is the true meaning of compassion. It enables us to recognize our profound interconnectedness with all beings . . . It is a measure of your humanity and your maturity. It is a measure of your open heart, and as your heart breaks open there will be room for the world to heal.

Joanna Macy

FACES OF THE
SACRED

Most high, omnipotent,
good Lord,
Thine are all praise, glory, honor and
all benedictions.
To Thee alone, Most High, do they belong
And no man is worthy to name Thee.

Praise be to Thee, My Lord, with all
Thy creatures,
Especially Brother Sun,
Who is our day and lightens us
therewith.
Beautiful is he and radiant with great
splendor;
Of Thee, Most High, he bears expression.

Praise be to Thee, my Lord, for
Sister Moon, and for the stars
In the heavens which Thou has formed
bright, precious and fair.

Praise be to Thee, my Lord, for
Brother Wind,
And for the air and the cloud of fair
and all weather
Through which Thou givest
sustenance to Thy creatures.

Praise be, my Lord, for Sister Water.
Who is most useful, humble, precious
and chaste.

Praise be, my Lord, for Brother Fire,
By whom Thou lightest up the night:
He is beautiful, merry, robust and strong.

Praise be, my Lord, for our sister,
Mother Earth,
Who sustains and governs us
And brings forth diverse fruits with
many-hued flowers and grass.

St. Francis of Assisi

I wake in a god!

I open my eyes. The god lifts from the water. His head fills the bay. He is Puget Sound, the Pacific; his breast rises from pastures, his fingers are firs, islands slide wet down his shoulders. Islands slip blue from his shoulders and glide over the water, the empty, lighted water like a stage.

Today's god rises, his long eyes flecked in clouds. He flings his arms, spreading colors; he arches, cupping sky in his belly, he vaults, vaulting and spreading, holding all and spread on me like skin.

Annie Dillard

The pale flowers of the dogwood outside this window are saints. The little yellow flowers that nobody notices on the edge of that road are saints looking up into the face of God.

This leaf has its own texture and its own pattern of veins and its own holy shape, and the bass and trout hiding in the deep pools of the river are canonized by their beauty and their strength.

The lakes hidden among the hills are saints, and the sea too is a saint who praises God without interruption in her majestic dance.

Thomas Merton

The purpose of the plant kingdom is to feed animals and humans, to hold the soil together, to enhance beauty, to balance the atmosphere. I was told the plants and trees sing to us humans silently, and all they ask in return is for us to sing to them.

Marlo Morgan

A tree gives glory to God by being a tree. For in being what God means it to be it is obeying Him. It "consents," so to speak, to His creative love. It is expressing an idea which is God and which is not distinct from the essence of God, and therefore a tree imitates God by being a tree.

Thomas Merton

What does God look like? These fish, this water, this land.

Linda Hogan

One thing we know for sure. The earth was not made for man, man was made for the earth.

Chief Seattle

When you are walking along a path leading into a village, you can practice mindfulness . . . If we're really engaged in mindfulness while walking along the path to the village, then we will consider the act of each step we take as an infinite wonder, and a joy will open our hearts like a flower, enabling us to enter the world of reality.

I like to walk alone on country paths, rice plants and wild grasses on both sides, putting each foot down on the earth in mindfulness, knowing that I walk on the wondrous earth. In such moments, existence is a miraculous and mysterious reality. People usually consider walking on water or in thin air a miracle. But I think the real miracle is not to walk either on water or in thin air, but to walk on earth.

Thich Nhat Hanh

It is autumn here and the golden leaves falling one by one are truly beautiful. Taking a ten-minute walk in the woods, watching my breath and maintaining mindfulness, I feel refreshed and restored. Like that, I can really enter into a communion with each leaf.

Thich Nhat Hanh

Spirituality
is not to be learned
by flight from the world
by running away from things,
or by turning solitary and going apart from the world.
Rather,
we must learn an inner solitude
wherever or with whomsoever we may be.
We must learn to penetrate things
and find God there.

Meister Eckhart

It was he who gave me true knowledge of all that is,
who taught me the structure of the world and the properties
    of the elements,
the beginning, end and middle of the times,
the alternation of the solstices and the succession of the seasons,
the revolution of the year and the positions of the stars,
the natures of animals and the instincts of wild beasts,
the powers of spirits and the mental process of men,
the varieties of plants and the medical properties of roots.
All that is hidden, all that is plain, I have come to know,
instructed by Wisdom who designed them all.

Wisdom 7: 17–21

What a thing it is to sit absolutely alone,
in the forest, at night, cherished by this
wonderful, unintelligible,
perfectly innocent speech,
the most comforting speech in the world,
the talk that rain makes by itself all over the ridges,
and the talk of the watercourses everywhere in the
hollows!
  Nobody started it, nobody is going to stop it.
It will talk as long as it wants, this rain.
As long as it talks I am going to listen.

Thomas Merton

The whole creation is eagerly waiting for God to reveal his sons and daughters. It was not for any fault on the part of creation that it was made unable to attain its purpose, it was made so by God; but creation still retains the hope of being freed, like us, from its slavery to decadence, to enjoy the same freedom and glory as the children of God. From the beginning till now the entire creation, as we know, has been groaning in the great act of giving birth; and not only creation, but all of us who possess the first-fruits of the Spirit, we too groan inwardly as we wait for our bodies to be set free.

Romans 8: 19–23

The natural world is the larger sacred community to which we belong. To be alienated from this community is to become destitute in all that makes us human. To damage this community is to diminish our own existence.

We need to know the great story of the universe in its four phases of emergence: the galactic story, the earth story, the life story, the human story.

Thomas Berry

The birds I heard today, which fortunately, did not come within the scope of my science, sang as freshly as if it had been the first morning of creation.

Henry David Thoreau

The universe is bound together in communion, each thing with all the rest. The gravitational bond unites all the galaxies; the electromagnetic interaction binds all the molecules; the genetic information connects all the generations of the ancestral tree of life. We live in interwoven layers of bondedness.

Brian Swimme

It is God whom human beings know in every creature.

Hildegard of Bingen

The day will come when, after mastering the wind, the waves, the tides and gravity, we shall harness for God the energies of love. And on that day, for the second time in the history of the world, humanity will have discovered fire.

Pierre Teilhard de Chardin

NOTES

INTRODUCTION

From *Up from Eden*. Copyright © 1981 by Ken Wilber. Used by permission of Doubleday, a division of Bantam Doubleday Dell Publishing Group, Inc.

TANGLED ROOTS

Thomas Merton, quoted by Matthew Fox in *A Spirituality Named Compassion*. Winston Press, 1979. Used by permission.

From *A Sand County Almanac*. Copyright © 1966 by Aldo Leopold. Used by permission of Oxford University Press, Inc.

From *The Golden String*. Copyright © 1980 by Bede Griffiths. Used by permission of the Bede Griffiths Trust, and of the Harvill Press.

From *The Sacred Pipe: Black Elk's Account of the Seven Rites of the Oglala Sioux*, 1953. Joseph Epes Brown, ed. Used by permission of the University of Oklahoma Press.

From "Creations," in *Heart of the Land: Essays on Last Great Places*. Joseph Barbato and Lisa Weinerman, eds. Copyright © 1994 by Linda Hogan. Used by permission of Pantheon Books.

EARTH LESSONS

ONE BODY

NOTES

From *The Book on the Taboo Against Knowing Who You Are*. Copyright © 1966 by Alan Watts. Copyright © 1966 by Alan Watts. Reprinted by permission of Pantheon Books.

From *Woman and Nature: The Roaring Inside Her*. Copyright © 1978 by Susan Griffin. Reprinted by permission of HarperCollins Publishers, Inc.

John Seed, cited by Bill Devall and George Sessions, *Deep Ecology: Living As If Nature Mattered*. Gibbs-Smith, Publisher (1985). Used by permission.

From *The Sacred Pipe: Black Elk's Account of the Seven Rites of the Oglala Sioux*, 1953. Joseph Epes Brown, ed. Used by permission of the University of Oklahoma Press.

From *The Dream of the Earth*. Copyright © 1988 by Thomas Berry. Used by permission of Sierra Club Books.

From *Let the Mountains Talk, Let the Rivers Run* by David Bower. Reprinted by permission of HarperCollins Publishers, Inc.

From *Small Is Beautiful*. Copyright © 1975 by E.F. Schumacher. Used by permission of HarperCollins Publishers, Inc.

From *The Dream of the Earth*. Copyright © 1988 by Thomas Berry. Used by permission of Sierra Club Books.

CALM WILDNESS

From "Wild Again" by Bill McKibben in *Heart of the Land: Essays on Last Great Places*. Joseph Barbato and Lisa Weinerman, eds. Used by permission of Pantheon Books.

Reprinted from *The Long Road Turns to Joy: A Guide to Walking Meditation* by Thich Nhat Hanh (1996) with permission of Parallax Press, Berkeley, California.

John Burroughs, cited in *John Burroughs' America*, edited by Farida A. Wiley, illustrated by Francis Lee Jaques. Used by permission of Devin-Adair Publishers.

WONDERS NEVER CEASE

NOTES

From *The Sense of Wonder*. Copyright © 1956 by Rachel L. Carson. Copyright © renewed 1984 by Roger Christie. Reprinted by permission of HarperCollins Publishers, Inc.

Grey Owl, from *Tales of an Empty Cabin*. Toronto: 1936. Used by permission of Macmillan of Canada.

From *Let the Mountains Talk, Let the Rivers Run* by David Bower. Reprinted by permission of HarperCollins Publishers, Inc.

From *The Universe Story*. Copyright © 1992 by Thomas Berry and Brian Swimme. Used by permission of HarperCollins Publishers, Inc.

From *Pilgrim at Tinker Creek*. Copyright © 1974 by Annie Dillard. Reprinted by permission of HarperCollins Publishers, Inc.

From *Dancing on the Shore* by Harold Horwood. Used by permission of McClelland & Stewart, Inc., Toronto, *The Canadian Publishers*.

From *Walden* by Henry David Thoreau. Reprinted by permission of Princeton University Press.

From *Pilgrim at Tinker Creek*. Copyright © 1974 by Annie Dillard. Reprinted by permission of HarperCollins Publishers, Inc.

From *Sitting Bull, Champion of the Sioux*, by Stanley Vestal. Used by permission of the University of Oklahoma Press.

From *Nature, Man and Woman*. Copyright © 1958 by Alan Watts. Used by permission of Random House, Inc.

From *Pilgrim at Tinker Creek*. Copyright © 1974 by Annie Dillard. Reprinted by permission of HarperCollins Publishers, Inc.

Mahabharata, cited in *Environmental Crisis and Hindu Religion* by O.P. Dwivedi. Used by permission of Gitanjali Publishing House, New Delhi, India.

LIVING WITH RESPECT

NOTES

From "Purity, Pollution, and Hinduism" by Linda Gupta in *Ecofeminism and the Sacred*. Carol Adams, ed. Used by permission of the Continuum Publishing Group.

From *Earth House Hold*. Copyright © 1969 by Gary Snyder. Reprinted by permission of New Directions Publishing Corp.

From *Pilgrim at Tinker Creek*. Copyright © 1974 by Annie Dillard. Reprinted by permission of HarperCollins Publishers, Inc.

From *The Dream of the Earth*. Copyright © 1988 by Thomas Berry. Used by permission of Sierra Club Books.

Excerpt from "Everything Is a Human Being" in *Living by the Word: Selected Writings 1973-1987*, copyright © 1984 by Alice Walker, reprinted by permission of Harcourt Brace & Company.

From *A Sand County Almanac*. Copyright © 1966 by Aldo Leopold. Used by permission of Oxford University Press, Inc.

From "The Memory Place" by Barbara Kingsolver in *Heart of the Land: Essays on Last Great Places*. Joseph Barbato and Lisa Weinerman, eds. Used by permission of Pantheon Books.

From *A Sand County Almanac*. Copyright © 1966 by Aldo Leopold. Used by permission of Oxford University Press, Inc.

From "Purity, Pollution, and Hinduism" by Linda Gupta in *Ecofeminism and the Sacred*. Carol Adams, ed. Used by permission of the Continuum Publishing Group.

Anonymous, cited in "Ethnology of the Fox Indians," by William Jones, *Bureau of American Ethnology Bulletin* 125 (1939).

Reprinted from *World as Lover, World as Self* by Joanna Macy (1991) with permission of Parallax Press, Berkeley, California.

FACES OF THE SACRED